PEOPLE ARE CRUEL

Only God is Good. Mark 10: 18

Karen Kellock Ph.D.

Manual for
Superior Men

**This is a complete theory based on Einstein physics,
Political Psychology, Systems Theory
and Archetypal Psychiatry.**

FORMULA

**All success attraction
All disease obstruction
All recovery elimination**

You must fast on all three

OBSTRUCTIONS:

**People
Habit
Food**

PEOPLE ARE CRUEL

Due to a lack of self-confidence you team with another and they ruin you, your business and your future.   The narcissist is all about smear campaigns so go no contact with them and all who listened to em. After the emotional cut-off there are no more symptoms--just that alone is proof of the sick system.   As people go more crazy [since evil is infinite and progressive] I'd say you should isolate.

CONSTANT ALERT

EFFECTS OF CONSTANT STRESS
SMV IS A CRUEL WEAPON
DEVIL TAKES OVER THE DOCILE
BULLY NARCISSISTIC FEMALES
VIEW HIM AS A SUCKING SNAKE
IT'S AN EMOTIONAL FAMINE
PROTEIN DEPRIVATION
FINAL FREEDOM
TELL THE WORLD THIS

CONSTANT ALERT

EFFECTS OF CONSTANT STRESS

It's a constant level of stress living with a narc. The body isn't designed to be triggered all the time.

The body's destroyed thru constant trauma. Once you leave it will be restored: no more drama.

Stress never stops: the fight or flight mechanism tires out and we collapse with no more clout.

Trauma after trauma to small or large things. You're driven insane then he just blames you see.

The alert system blasts constantly, it ever stops. The emotions are shredded, all energy drops.

The body is not designed by God to react to such threats all the time so it finally collapses, aye.

Forgiving them is the only way to disconnect from them. See it that way and it's easier man.

Each day you avoid him contributes to your flowering as the demon eclipsed your true self hourly.

Hooked by the trauma he caused you evoking chemicals you're then addicted to. Whew.

Narcissist abuse damages the brain see. Confusion, indecision and slow processing. Cure: LEAVE.

Enough is enough. Leave the narcissist and get your brain back. Don't minimize this, it's a fact.

SMV IS A CRUEL WEAPON

CONSTANT ALERT

Cruel men use ageism as weapon. That's the concept of SMV: it's cold and cruel, used to bludgeon.

That's why the old sequester into retirement communities, to avoid remarks/ageist cruelty.

SMV is part of the "unfair comparisons" syndrome of abuse, as if we're all alike/judged by fools.

To be treated that way due to age or gender was frightening like as if I didn't exist sir.

Don't take SMV to heart and from any man talking like that, depart. Your value is not by perverts.

I'm retired from a cruel world so why continue it online? It's cold, discounting, no friends of mine.

An unboundaried woman is like taking candy from a baby. Evil flows in without restraint/heavy.

Don't let a man in your house and you'll save yourself years of remorse for they take over of course.

DEVIL TAKES OVER THE DOCILE

There are now as many female as male narcissists and they are real bitches. Be leery and resist.

Narcissistic abuse is the devil taking over the docile. See the signs and remove yourself NOW.

Narcissistic abuse is a killing of the soul by a grandiose phony who doesn't love you at all.

Add it up what he gave you, it's nothing. But you're still enthralled and hooked by bread crumbing.

Pride goeth before the fall you know. Life can change suddenly Joe, let the grandiose arrogance go.

CONSTANT ALERT

You'll always have opposition--the adversary--so why take it personally? Expect it and dig in.

The alert can't stomach grandiosity of the jerk but the pop are dumbed down/have lost concern.

BULLY NARCISSISTIC FEMALES

I felt opposition every time I met a woman. Many men too but they're less like a pit viper's venom.

The alpha female is surrounded by her flying monkeys who do her bidding. They are her hit men.

The narcissistic alpha female targets an odd girl out--the strange one refusing to conform/adapt.

I had **MANY** bully females come after me, including bully females in my own family see.

If you find em cruel in divorce courts you oughta see what they do to females who won't conform.

I was always the odd girl out so suffered female opposition all my life, and men too, aye.

I join no cults or fan clubs. They are sickening as a grandiose phony gets a herd's mass love.

An online dyad can be just as destructive as if he's here with you in your room. See that/drop fools.

With collagen the body composition of fat to muscle changes and you weigh more--forget it all.

The more you avoid him the more you come outa your shell, feeling worthless after a narc's spell.

VIEW HIM AS A SUCKING SNAKE

CONSTANT ALERT

View him as a snake sucking the life out of you. A giant python aiming to make you miserable too.

He's dashing, he's clever--but thus is the brilliant beauty of LUCIFER. See thru images/return.

For every time you stay away from him you get closer to your own goal. Remember that always, go.

I've had narc abuse, I've been addicted to crumbs making me even more obsessed with a bum.

I know how narcissistic abuse works. They're all alike, it's like a machine and you get hooked.

Just like with apathetic parents, you are content with one complement in a sea of invalidation.

IT'S AN EMOTIONAL FAMINE

You get used to living in emotional famine. A drought which is mental and spiritual: very unlovin'

Let God bring you to the fore, not gimmicks for fame & glory--that only comes from God/assured.

Narcissists: they're all alike, it works like a machine: we get hooked [trauma bonded] by the mean.

You won't ever get canceled for being too woke. You can say men can have babies you know.

At some point he becomes stone cold in essence, having no more need of your presence.

Once they're done with you they treat you as their biggest enemy--you're now a stranger see.

It was just a facade but now there's no need for the "emotional attachment" that never was.

CONSTANT ALERT

Narcissist attachment disorder: Can't attach to you in a healthy way but can't detach either ok.

The narcissist will go no-contact once you start saying "NO!". That shuts him down you know.

EVERYTHING is about him. This is the core feature of the narcissist and to you it's destruction.

PROTEIN DEPRIVATION

Protein: you don't need a lot of it but need it throughout the day to properly absorb it ok.

Within a week of animal fat/protein-only with collagen the skin smoothes out: it's normal again.

Without protein/collagen holding the skin together, it gets weaker, wrinkled and wholly irregular.

Without protein you see dry patches, lines, wrinkles, discolorations; WITH protein it won't happen.

The skin gets so dry you feel a prisoner in your own body. I kept putting the moisturizers on all day.

A slice of cheese is an easy way to get it and it's nice cuz it satiates too see. A little bit is all you need.

There's an easy way to solve "not getting enough to eat": eat a piece of cheese, it serves our needs.

I'm not a big eater, I never eat enough and forget about food. Eating mouse meals of protein is cool.

You will now have shine, health and vigor. You can do the things you've planned to do for years.

I eat vegetables but it's not the predominant thing anymore, it's PROTEIN holding things together.

CONSTANT ALERT

FINAL FREEDOM

Now I'm retired on my own land, I earned it man. I'm a free woman, outa the social matrix of demons.

I love the dirt, I lay in the sun, I thank God every minute for freedom after being pulled in all directions.

Freedom also means no online distractions and trauma bonds. Get offa that thing/avoid wrong.

If you feel unblessed, check your environment. You won't be blessed around mockers/gossipers.

You'll never have anything greater than the environment you're in. Check the environment children.

He's the closest thing to God, brilliant—just ask him. But in truth he's a raging dirtball who gets bored again.

He's the closest thing to God—just ask him. But in truth he's a raging dirt-ball who gets bored again.

The truth is the narcissist is a closed minded idiot and abusive scum throwing out breadcrumbs.

God prepares you for right relationships son--by giving you strength/savvy to reject wrong ones.

TELL THE WORLD THIS

Climate change politix is the biggest money maker ever and making it a moral issue is most clever.

It was black Africans & Arabians who sold blacks into slavery. The whites only participated partially.

CRUELTY DESCRIBED

I WANT YOU ARMORED
THE LOUD CROWD
PREPARE FOR DISASTER/HAVE SUCCESS
HELL ON EARTH: OUR WAR
SILLY WOMEN
THE SUCKING SPIRIT
WHEN THE HEDGE IS DOWN
DISENGAGE IF THEY WALK YOU BY
SOCIETIES DOMINATED BY ENVY
AGE MAGNIFIES WEAKNESS
START WEEKEND FAST ON WEDNESDAY
FAST TO BE A KNIGHT
CANNIBIS GONE CRAZY

CRUELTY DESCRIBED

I WANT YOU ARMORED

The world will beat you up and take you down. I want you armored, prepared to take the crown.

It is correct to be defensive, even paranoid. That's the correct stance for Christians/God anoints.

Socialization teaches empathy, civility and emotional regulation so what happens with isolation?

Modern liberals trust too easily. They chum up immediately and that's always confused me.

I can't stand silly women cuz they're not funny but MEAN if something doesn't agree with em.

I know what it's like driven crazy/misjudged horribly. To vindicate self I had to write an entire theory.

He allowed me to decline into my psychosis but when it got so bad dumped me because of it.

"If we took out all the offensive parts there'd be nothing left". Liberal publisher to KK.

THE LOUD CROWD

The loud crowd accuses us of being standoffish but separation is holy and we've a high level of disgust.

Much more need be said of the cruelty of people. That way we're walled and can stay joyful.

Never trust appearances. See that sweet lady over there? She's really a scorpion miss.

CRUELTY DESCRIBED

The world will hammer you when you're up and when you're down. Be ready and take the crown.

They hate us for our disgust. We draw lines and love repentance while they love the unjust.

Get confidence up so high that nothing can hurt you cuz you know exactly who you are: a star.

Be ready for the insults coming from jealousy and envy which is totally predictable honey.

Her high school friends hated her for her beautiful singing voice so she relocated: good choice.

Your best friends can turn and pull you down, Divulging/leaking confidences all over town.

Your own mother can work to destroy your reputation for life. We have to stop seeing images, aye.

"They hated me when I was fat and hated me when I lost weight". David Goggins

PREPARE FOR DISASTER/HAVE SUCCESS

Forget all the invader did, just be grateful how you escaped him--the other's taken for granted.

I escaped a WAR and that war was you and you and you. The relocation gave me freedom too.

Retirement is: freedom from people officiously telling you what to do or spreading rumors too.

I came out of a social war with people invading me constantly until I relocated/laid boundaries.

I still have PTSD intrusive memories of a buncha dummies invading me with no remedy.

CRUELTY DESCRIBED

Suddenly I related far more to the ELEMENTS: the whisper of wind, a balmy breeze, the crickets.

The elemental reality was soothing/reassuring there's something higher than what I was seeing.

I'm not worried cuz I'm fully protected now see--in my worldview that's MATURITY/boundaries.

HELL ON EARTH: OUR WAR

But down the ladder it was hell on earth and just thinking about it makes me shudder.

Nothing to complain about, it wasn't a real war just a social one but what it did was destruction.

Once you repent the old life is over forever and the black cloud disperses along with users.

The more you think you need em the bigger they appear but when whole that disappears.

They try to copy you and it's pathetic. Unwilling to do the work you did they're jealous plagiarists.

They copy your style but don't have the character to pull it off. Don't worry they're all fluff.

SILLY WOMEN

If they don't agree not only will they reject you but ruin your reputation too: the female crew.

Unreliable people who make plans and break em are dangerous, making you crooked just to adapt.

When obstructed you can't get nourishment. There's no assimilation or elimination, you're a mess.

CRUELTY DESCRIBED

She fleshed out to what you allowed. You said she's always beau so forget exercising the bod.

Anachronism: something that's dead but refuses to be laid to rest. Belonging to another era, alas.

Debunk, reconstruct: We empty cup in order to refill it with a new matrix which changes our luck.

THE SUCKING SPIRIT

He represents a sucking spirit. You lay a boundary and he'll bust it then take everything within it.

The effects of things is age-dependent. Suddenly you can't take "medical marijuana" like you did.

Those edibles are the devil. I can't tell you how many times I called 911 in a panic of hell. Lady

They call it medical marijuana but it will getcha in a trip to the ER in a terrified dystopian trauma.

Cannabis gummies: Could you have a bad trip from a mere lick? YES, and not just a little kick.

When fasting I don't react to chemicals or pet dander but when eating it's such a dam downer.

A quart of orange juice a day and ice cream in the am, get it? The sugar diet and I'm high as a kite.

It takes ten days to recover from a "gummy bad trip" but the MJ head said "what if I just licked it?"

One time you did not react and you've won the pot of gold. Smash neuropathways and be bold.

There was a hellish time they had power over me and now I see they were for Hillary.

CRUELTY DESCRIBED

There's a conspiracy against privacy in social or familial cultures and false churches.

Home should be something you always wanna return to not avoid cuz she picks fights with you.

WHEN THE HEDGE IS DOWN

When the hedge is down even people who don't want to will come against you hon'.

The better an envious man is treated the worse he gets. He sees it as you superior/against.

Giving to someone like that makes him feel humiliated like you're above him so you donated.

The beneficiary can never absolve himself of the memory that the gift was an act of charity.

There were enviers doubting sincerity of the Marshall Plan to rebuild Europe-- what's the hook?

Angry dependence: the more you help em the more they hate you, later seeking vengeance.

DISENGAGE IF THEY WALK YOU BY

When people walk you by and have many others in their life, disengage and see it as a sign.

She was the most vicious rep-destroyer I've ever met yet everyone saw her as nice as it gets.

Dependency Theory: America's abundance is the cause of poverty in the rest of the world see.

The advantages obtained by the rich were only at others expense: that's their political sense.

CRUELTY DESCRIBED

In some places doing favors is rare/creates suspicion. Kindness to outsiders is looked down on.

Don't preemptively give stuff away to prevent envy, just be bold enough to defy it see.

Some men with strong hearts are not intimidated by envy of others, they just ignore the losers.

The anti-racists don't nurture by teaching skills or how to defer gratification for the future.

"You have less cuz the white man has more by rigging the game in his own favor": liberal lore.

SOCIETIES DOMINATED BY ENVY

Many societies were dominated by envy but few like the rising generation of nonwhites see.

Then there's white guilt for having more then the sweating masses: the giving is ridiculous.

The deliberate cultivation of racial guilt and resentment is seen in CRT or communism.

The only beneficiaries of critical race theory will be the powerful, it's just division to make em full.

To understand the social effects of envy just live in a small liberal town with the hornets buzzing.

Envy happens by proximity. Physical or social separation diminishes it so I escaped see.

The Big Don hands out money to all so they won't be jealous of him, his money and his castle.

They're even jealous of our hard work: Working to get ahead brings just as much envy/hatred.

CRUELTY DESCRIBED

New reality: 5 black cops beating a black man to death is white supremacy and no-cops is safety.

The government scorns us as they tax us for the benefit of people who despise us.

State of Union was all on advantageous issues but not the actual and appalling decline too.

AGE MAGNIFIES WEAKNESS

As she aged any weakness was magnified when she deviated in her diet proven to work, aye.

Since my weekend starts on Wednesday the weekend fast is five days to Monday. Vaca = happy!

The fast shifts gears, opens up new windows, reveals new viewpoints while God always anoints.

The fast gives reason for new hope. Stuck in old routines some lose courage/resort to dope.

I look at weekend fasts as vacation or entering an inner realm which says "enter here, not a tear".

Intrusive thoughts at the worst times: this kind of junk inside is gone with weekend fast [days = 5].

Fast for PTSD: wipe it out, wipe it clean. God gave us a way to erase the past and come up again.

I LOVE the feeling of getting a fresh start, granted another chance, wiping the slate clean again.

Silly women terrified at idea of going without food. Like as if they know anything plus they're rude.

No orange juice on the fast. Just water if anything but it's best to dry fast-- imbibe zero, nothing.

CRUELTY DESCRIBED

START WEEKEND FAST ON WEDNESDAY

Start weekend fast on wednesday and turn phone off. This is your VACA to your destiny: blastoff.

If studying something on the fast, you'll zero in on it and become ONE with it/it's such a blast.

Work out on the fast because HGH [Human Growth Hormone] is triggered then = de-aging.

Because you wanna stay in this new exciting realm you won't give into hunger should it overwhelm.

God put me on a fast for ten days and there was not one pang of hunger: isn't He a Wonder?

For those who fear effects of aging, fasting is the way I'll say again [and years are added from sin]

You'll resemble a shiny carved child, totally creative and way above the food-obsessed crowd.

FAST TO BE A KNIGHT

Complete the fast [as YOU vowed] and you're a knight. Overcoming self is the true strength, aye.

Be specific on what you want. I said books success and lotsa money Lord and I mean much.

It's exciting, an opportunity—so start to see it that way. Embark on this journey with me to agree.

It's like a big magic balloon taking you up and away from your problems and life's complexities.

Forgiveness comes easier when unobstructed with food for modern substances are irritators.

CRUELTY DESCRIBED

As the past breaks down like a bad dream it disperses to be replaced by the no-past FUTURE.

The morbid past is maintained by a rigid infrastructure of DEBRIS which keeps us rememberin' see.

Most debris is fecal matter, retained water and uneliminated foods maintaining memory sir.

Break down the physical obstruction and the memory is gone: herein is the mind-body connection.

CANNIBIS GONE CRAZY

It's one puff for the day, not smoke all day. But this kinda finesse the pothead doesn't have ok.

One puff: if you get scared you know it'll die down soon. But with edibles it's all unknown Sue.

Two puffs? Learn to say NO. Three puffs? HELL NO. Four puffs? Call 911/the whole day's blown.

The dispensary products are STRONG. We must relearn the ropes cuz we've done it all wrong.

Don't mix with stimulants like coffee or tea, don't mix with other products and delimit sugar.

Since pot went legal many people call 911 and the medicals. It's ONE PUFF and forget edibles!

Regarding your work, if it's perfect God will bring attention to it. Now relax and complete it.

Regarding all obstructions, it was God shaping me the whole time. That's cuz He's the Potter, aye.

PEOPLE ARE CRUEL

Only God is Good. Mark 10: 18

NARCISSIST SMEAR CAMPAIGNS
HENPECKING STARTING
FALSE SELF IMAGE
ANGER AT YOUR BOUNDARIES
WHITE PRIVILEGE CRAP
THE LONELY & BORED LOVE TV
MENTAL ILLNESS & SELF-AWARENESS
GOING TO WAR ON SLIGHTS
IN THE MIDST OF EVIL
SELF-FORGIVENESS
SELF-FORGIVENESS FOR GREATNESS
DON'T LET EM HANG OUT
POSTWAR LOW KEY
MOVE PAST FAILURES
IT'S INCREDIBLE LOOKING BACK
SELF-FORGIVE TO REDEFINE YOURSELF
WOMEN PUSH HUSBANDS LEFT
SELF-FORGIVENESS
ADRASTIC CHANGE IN LOOKS/ARCHETYPE
THE LOVING MERCHANTS OF MISERY
COLLECTIVE INTUITION IS INFECTIOUS
GENIUS HAS FEW FRIENDS
NO EVIL CONTRACTS
DIVIDE FROM THE CRASS/GROSS HERD
NOT JUST DOING BUT CONDONING

PEOPLE ARE CRUEL

Only God is Good. Mark 10: 18

FACE CRUELTY OR PAINT A FALSE REALITY
FEMINISTS THINK IT'S COOL TO DOMINATE
THE NEW TOLERANCE MAKES US POWERLESS
NEW AGERS ARE INTELLECTUAL RUNTS
NEW AGE UTOPIA IS REALLY HELL
GO WITH TRENDIES OR REALITY OF CENTURIES?
MORAL VIEWPOINT IS DIVISIVE: THIS IS GOOD
RESISTANCE TO GENIUS IS ENORMOUS
LIBERALISM IS NOT FREEDOM
"EVIL DOESN'T EVEN EXIST"
LIBERALS AND FALSE COMPASSION
THE WINNING SMILE IN SUPERFICIAL GENERATIONS
GENDER AND MARRIAGE
UNDER STRESS THEY REGRESS
QUEEN BEES AND DOMINATRICES
WITH CRISES GO TO GOD NOT THE MOB
DUMB OR BRAINWASHED TO HATE FREEDOM?
GOD AND GUNS GO TOGETHER
ENVIRONMENTALISM SEEKS POWER
IF CONTROLLED BY GROUPTHINK YOU'RE A WIMP
POPULARITY: NO RELATION TO TRUTH
UPPITY STARDOM SEEKERS
PROMISCUOUS, FRIVOLOUS, DESTRUCTIVE AND INANE
SOCIAL HARLOTS AND THE RED CARPET

PEOPLE ARE CRUEL
Only God is Good. Mark 10: 18

NON-GENIUSES SEEK APPROVAL
DUMB PUT SMART DOWN
LOVE THE HOOD BUT HATE THE GOOD
HATRED OF TRADITION IS DARK LIKE SLUM
BORING LOQUACITY NOT DEEP THOUGHT
MEDIUM CHILL: CORDIAL BUT STEEL
MESSED UP B WEAK MEN/ANGRY WOMEN
RAMPANT MALE SUICIDE
IMAGE-MAGICIANS
LOVE YOUR SPOUSE: IT'S A CHOICE
TRANSCEND LEVITY
THE HERD IS CONSENSUAL BLINDNESS
SLAVERY WAS EVERYWHERE
FEMINISTS ARE THE CRUELEST
THEY WANT US TO HATE OUR HERITAGE
MY GHOST TOWN
DIDN'T WANNA LEAVE A SHACK
UNWELCOME INTRUDERS
WRITERS AND ISOLATION
I WANT CLASS AND VALUES
ONE LITTLE [HUGE] LIFE CHANGE
BASIS OF AMERICANA: RIGHTS
HYERSENSTIVITY UPDATES
HAPPY UPDATES

PEOPLE ARE CRUEL

Only God is Good. Mark 10: 18

NARCISSIST SMEAR CAMPAIGNS

The narcissist is all about smear campaigns so go no contact with them and all who listened to em.

LIFE: Imagine you've a beautiful mansion then someone brings it all down with their sinnin'.

Sociopath idea of right/wrong: right is what I want now and wrong is when someone says no.

The flip side of the daughter of misfortune is the queen having learned all the pertinent lessons.

First I was the new kid on the block now I own the whole block, what do you think of that chump?

Teen murders are up and it's all about jealousy & the communist spirit: "he has more than me."

Getting involved with people is a form of slavery as they maintain the status quo/it's like a jail.

HENPECKING STARTING

The henpecking started when I splashed into Borrego and gossip spreads like cancer ya know.

They always need something and if you're a good guy they'll soak you dry but life's a pie.

I have no real friends and everyone is bad, what do you think of that? Man has two sides: fact.

PEOPLE ARE CRUEL

I can sense the vacuity of something so it just makes me sick when you bloviate, faking.

When getting involved means locking you in that's gone too far for a creative, be careful friend.

Narcissist psychopath always chooses revenge over reconciliation, oneupmanship over you man.

To the narcissist you're not a name but a function. What an insanity-maker of destruction.

FALSE SELF IMAGE

He has to live behind image the false self has created for him even if it means turning on friends.

My own husband suddenly shifted gears into destroying me completely. Narcissist survivor

Covert narcissist is ALL about virtue signaling to appear all-ok and that's the most prevalent today.

Narcissist controls how its seen or interpreted--you will be nuts after a while in that predicament.

You're not even a name to him but a function. This too is a crazy-maker like you don't exist hon'

It's not just getting away from him, you're better off totally outside his sphere of influence hon'.

His smear campaign is ruinous but the psychologically lazy lets it pass by, never asking you why.

So now everywhere you go is a black cloud from his smear campaign, lifted when you relocate.

ANGER AT YOUR BOUNDARIES

PEOPLE ARE CRUEL

All she knows is you won't let her take over your house and she's gonna get you good for it now.

All he knows is you're not giving him attention anymore. Once he got it he'd discredit you even more.

It does not matter whether he's old or young, the sociopathic tendencies are that strong.

Mean and stubborn: He's got a short fuse or he's not even listening to her, a fighter not a lover.

She even threatened me with her vengeance and I knew what that meant: she'd start her gossip.

She even said if I "did that again" she'd "really retaliate" and that's how she held court every day.

I was leery the whole time of social hypnosis and its homeostatic devices to make me conform.

It's all about retaliation not reconciliation--they're too superior to you to ever reconcile hon'.

Intimate violence: you're more likely to lose your life to someone you know than a stranger, alas.

Intimate crimes require this passion-driven thing called attachment trauma and that'll kill ya.

She appears to give a complement when actually she's insulting you and she's so good at it.

WHITE PRIVILEGE CRAP

Sister accused me of having white privilege in the sixties and for many neurotic decades I felt guilty.

The blacks got mansions and the whites were consigned to a shabby cabin followed by guilt-trippin'.

PEOPLE ARE CRUEL

She decided to hate me and spread horrific stories in a smear campaign since I was white ok.

Don't blame them [the culprit] cuz you didn't know the ropes--that everyone's bad or on dope.

Don't blame them cuz you trusted without a fence. God's punishment was removing the hedge.

A narcissist wants to isolate her for control and restricts her from having any close friends at all.

THE LONELY & BORED LOVE TV

The lonely and bored love to have the TV on cuz it fills the house with noise to feel they belong.

Complete debauchery in Berlin in the 20's was followed by total tyranny in the thirties-forties.

Being rich is very isolating anywhere the communist spirit prevails. To escape envy, set sail.

You work hard all your life for the home/what you want and they hate you for it, refusing to work.

No you cannot have an RV hookup, not if you spend half the time in my house. Privacy please/class.

No you cannot have an RV hookup if you come here to charge your phone/use the john bud.

You're the foreman, maestro, conductor or contractor. YOU have attention to detail or it's over.

Sometimes I question our relationship when there's disparity but course that's true of anybody.

Most people are too psychologically lazy to check out the smear. They let it go by/tuck it away far.

PEOPLE ARE CRUEL

Just close the door then they can't argue with you about your needs for privacy--keeping them out!

Female creators always gain the rep of never being satisfied and the work suffers she cried.

Having been brainwashed they think entirely differently and there is no solution I'm sorry to say.

They don't think logically or with common sense but according to a whole different narrative.

One reason to relocate is the people have you so pegged and they don't wanna let you up.

Unless it's an exact replica of my design my whole body lurches in rebellion/I'm ready to retire hon'.

MENTAL ILLNESS & SELF-AWARENESS

A major part of mental illness is lack of self-awareness about it. Anosognosia they call it.

I walked around in a terrified, homesick fog for decades cuz no one ever primed me for this God.

Since biggest killer/ager is stress & people are the usual cause solitude extends our life with God.

It's not that women ghost men but women are not to CHASE men/feels like withdrawn attention.

Any woman different from the others and they'll get out their magnifier to flush out her flubbers.

They have a huge investment in you staying down cuz their identity is in relation to you as clown.

Life is hell cuza the other people in it. Left to our own we're never lonely or bored and I love it.

PEOPLE ARE CRUEL

They have an **IDENTITY** investment in keeping you down so recovery isn't easy cuza who's around.

Without adequate parenting you'll be trained by the brutal cold world instead and it's **BAD.**

GOING TO WAR ON SLIGHTS

She'd go to war on some supposed slight. Just when things were tranquil she'd pick a fight.

People in evil generations are outrageously imposing and without parents taught by life's hard lessons.

To go back is horrible--not to what I did but what I witnessed in this adulterous generation.

The war was terrible but the moral disintegration afterwards caused havoc eternal.

After witnessing hell in the war with dead bodies everywhere it changes your behavior.

But the next generation was spoiled and debauchery always follows. This was hell from below.

About us: educated about what liberals will use against us while remaining pure in motives.

IN THE MIDST OF EVIL

In the midst of evil we're seeing the power of the people. It always happens this way: rise, eagle!

There's been a turnaround: a comeback from the brink. God's returning us to the pink as government shrinks.

We must get the word out--that everything's in reverse: The world talks sweet but its a curse.

PEOPLE ARE CRUEL

Due to a lack of self-confidence you team with another and they ruin you, your business and your future.

After the emotional cut-off there were no more symptoms. Just that alone is proof of the sick system.

They don't wanna abolish the police, they wanna take em over with uniformed SJW's running the place.

I'm relying totally on **DESTINY** and the pull of God for I trust His plan, I believe He has one and I'm going for it man.

As people go more crazy [since evil is infinite and progressive] I'd say you should isolate.

SELF-FORGIVENESS

This awful sense of self-disgust is passed on: toxic shame. It's the human condition you hate.

The only reason he came over was to argue with me and get me to think just like him, dumbed.

The sisters laid evil seeds with everyone in town so when I got there it was like entering a bus-saw.

Of course they believed two sisters about me, there was two of em and truth lies with the majority.

She would gossip to haters and get real chummy with em. Envious women just loved the collusion.

Never let people just hang out. You worked to have a home--an accomplishment, they did not.

SELF-FORGIVENESS FOR GREATNESS

God has put greatness in you but it's being held captive by your inability to forgive yourself too.

PEOPLE ARE CRUEL

The inability to self-forgive is a demonic stronghold to keep the best of you buried/getting old.

We can't find the best versions of self until we self-forgive and remove the evil power from hell.

You can't shame a person who's self-forgiven and knows exactly how it comes from God and His Son.

A person who's self-forgiven doesn't live to prove anything to anyone--it's all done due to the Son.

I am comfortable with me/my story which I've chosen to inform me with lessons and wisdom see.

I'm not gonna be stuck in a pig's trough where I'm not supposed to be cuz I can't forgive myself.

To forgive yourself you pack up your past, put it away then make room to move into a new season.

Never convince em to stay. You need a podium to tell the world what to think so stay out of the fray.

Looking back it couldn't have been any other way. It was a lower life phase and you were unsaved.

DON'T LET EM HANG OUT

They just wanna hang out. If they're too long in your house you will hate them. Prov. 25: 17

Seldom set foot in your neighbor's house--too much of you, and they will hate you. Prov 25: 17

Don't let people take up precious time for each moment is divine if not cluttered by the swine.

To be victimized by small town gossip is like being caught in a bus-saw or a rip tide/horrendous ordeal.

PEOPLE ARE CRUEL

The biggest reason they robbed you more than money was to show you who's who by your loss.

When the only food that doesn't cause you pain is fruit, you're now a fruitarian by default.

Having PTSD is not being weak it's just how the brain works. It waits until safety to reveal truth.

Self-forgiveness is necessary for greatness and hating yourself keeps you down as servants.

In the female community it's all collusion: two against one, ever balancing forces thru talkin'

POSTWAR LOW KEY

Postwar era was so low key of course they were shocked with open debauchery in offspring.

A prison camp run by guards who jointly hate you and wanna make life hell for you too.

It's an interactional consciousness: a contagion of lunacy. Folie a deux, a famille or three.

The post-war era was the Grey Suit Era of low key after seeing what no one should ever see.

PTSD: You don't experience the event until later in safety, I guess to save the brain from collapsing.

Can't get you outa my mind you little demon. You're 30 years older so it should be dissolvin'

Broken record: Stop over-explaining you clod and stop using me as a data dump I might add.

This is toxic shame--hereditary. It's what we hide from with various crutches turned deadly.

PEOPLE ARE CRUEL

As long as your life is cluttered with your negative history you will never move into your destiny see.

Be like a mover: Pack up your history--pack it up TIGHT--so you can move on into your great destiny.

MOVE PAST FAILURES

When we don't move past failures we're unprepared to receive winds of change when they come.

Tho' a perfectionist there was a day I confronted my own humanity--my failures, that's how it works.

I had to see I was NOT my failures and those failures did NOT define me--they were another entity.

Then God said He'd use everything I had gone thru to bring me to the place He'd predestined.

Now I'd help other people who were traversing this terrain of people spitting in your face and dismay.

I finally forgave myself to the point people's judgments honestly don't matter for God did anoint.

God's forgiveness gives us freedom after wanting acceptance by people/groups/false religion.

You did it, you made the mistake but now you must move forward with your life/relocate.

How long will you crucify yourself for experiences you've had living as a normal human being?

With self-forgiveness we empty ourselves of the guilt holding us captive to the dead past.

These things create guilt, a debilitating mind set paralyzing the ability to change/they're stuck.

PEOPLE ARE CRUEL

IT'S INCREDIBLE LOOKING BACK

Ironically, guilt is the reason we can't break the soul tie due to shame over having sexual relations.

You can't believe it, you sunk to a new low, you're better than this but just sick in the head ya' know.

The guilt is like waist-deep quicksand! It won't kill you but won't allow you to move forward man.

You settle for the soul tie because your guilt won't allow you to see yourself as worthy of better.

There is no greater example of self-forgiveness and radical change than the apostle Paul.

Paul went from persecuting the church to being persecuted FOR the church much like us.

Paul's drastic change was based on the ability to forgive himself for ALL he had done so do it hon'.

Paul put to rest everything in the past while he reached forward to those things in front to be had.

Those who can't move forward can't see themselves differently. No self-love without forgiveness.

Guilt won't allow self-love--seeing self differently from the past--so one is stuck with no changes.

When God changed the fallen heart of man he did it with love. You'll never change until you love you.

You not forgiving me has nothing to do with me forgiving myself, I will not be held captive to hell.

Self-forgiveness gives us the opportunity to redefine ourselves and what a relief from old shells.

PEOPLE ARE CRUEL

SELF-FORGIVE TO REDEFINE YOURSELF

What you see here is a redefinition of me which couldn't have happened if I didn't forgive myself see.

Trumpism means: GREAT trade deals, not giving everything away free or allowing steals.

Self-style is the greatest artistry and we reject cancel culture, as Americans we are independent.

Democrats are vicious, smart and they do one thing: they always stick together. President Trump

Covid didn't crush the economy, government crushed the economy. Kristi Noem ripping Biden

Freedom is better than tyranny. We are exceptional and no one should apologize for that. Gov. Noem

The left takes its visions very seriously--more seriously than the rights of the people. Kristi. Noem

To not self-forgive spits in His face because we know what He went through to give us this.

WOMEN PUSH HUSBANDS LEFT

Women push their husbands to the left. This is a most dangerous trend so tell men not to let it.

Abandon your beliefs or shut down. That's what it's come to and America's on the edge mom.

The "Equality Act" brings the greatest inequality of the day while eroding all religious freedom ok.

Other misnomers: The War on Poverty was actually a war on African-American nuclear families.

PEOPLE ARE CRUEL

Democrats said "No man would ever say he was a woman just to get money and scholarships".

I don't know why God chose me to be the vessel for this Creative Act, a lifelong blessing in fact.

In a chain reaction of bought and paid for, that's Cancel Culture--whittling us down to commie censor.

Of course the cops got wind of things in a small town like from Liquor Store Linda his daily BJ.

By forgiving yourself it means you don't go back. Instead you wrap it up, forgive it, don't discuss it.

Ok you did it. Through the savior's death you are forgiven. Now you forget about it even.

SELF-FORGIVENESS

A person cannot change or move forward until they see themselves differently on the inside.

I would never see myself differently as long as I held myself to former failures: gotta let it go.

They base their forgiveness on self on how OTHERS forgive them, but "all have sinned." John 8: 4-11

Go and sin no more: Jesus says God has already forgiven you so with your life, move forward.

Your heavenly father--the Almighty/Creator--has already forgiven you so now ignore accusers.

Once you've repented He turns his wrathful attention on your accusers and brings them down.

In my desert solitude invasions were infrequent but when they came it was a disastrous moment.

PEOPLE ARE CRUEL

After being alone and finding my own reality, any social was an evil onslaught and I hated it totally.

I didn't want them in my tiny cabin! I was used to being alone, this was hell on earth man.

They seemed like they were lunging at me, wanting to own me or a piece me and it's hellish see.

There's a drastic change in your looks, attitude and archetype evoked if you're unequally yoked.

ADRASTIC CHANGE IN LOOKS/ARCHETYPE

It's a drastic change in your looks, attitude and archetype evoked from dietary change alone.

They were lunging at me, open caverns/bottomless pits of evil, in my own little desert cabin see.

Had it been a trailer I lived in the panic woulda been even worse but this taught me I needed a fence.

What did this fall into sin get us? The democrats--and ruthlessness. Globalism, pay to play, graft.

You swam in muddy waters, you literally didn't know any better. Amazing isn't it, realizing after.

I shook for five years after their invasion. It was so imposing I can't even describe it son.

2nd marriage was first time I felt protected in life. The first was a porous boundary/social guy.

I wanna be behind a man, not in front. The world is too much for me/I just wanna stay home son.

Hype & Spin: They're in a trance because only those in a trance would believe something like this.

PEOPLE ARE CRUEL

They call depopulation "health care" so you must always look for euphemisms like this: beware.

THE LOVING MERCHANTS OF MISERY

The "loving" are merchants of misery as they socially scheme and bash your dreams: they are mean!

Evil brings itself down: by creating crises the truth is exposed then our narrative shines for victory won.

Political correctness is cultural suicide. It's a lie we can perpetually backslide and throw lines aside.

Despite the scandals they're seen as awesome. It's a land without justice as we race to the bottom.

It's the social world vs. God, okay? Even churches are getting chatty instead of silent prayer on Sunday.

The "animating contest" is repeatedly challenging the evil, building more character after each level.

COLLECTIVE INTUITION IS INFECTIOUS

Collective intuition is infectious: In times of great evil that spark of divinity comes through like an eagle.

Not only is government not the answer it's the worst possible answer.

There is no individual thought just a list we're to believe in: automatically you know it's a lie/sin.

Someone writes a book then we have a whole new worldview and vocabulary seen as reality.

You cannot survive in a sea of humanity turning liberal after propagandized by public schools.

Let em all go they're not worthy to know they walked you by but heading below.

PEOPLE ARE CRUEL

How can you have a decent family if you don't draw lines. Yet they hate our Christian refinement.

The herd will justify anything--and that's the collective descent into the fiery pits and having raging fits.

When everyone's a monster and they lie/cheat and steal, all I think of is Jesus' great appeal.

The people are such idiots the way they let freedom go--more interested in sex and food, ya know.

GENIUS HAS FEW FRIENDS

For I have very few friends. I don't have time for I just want home, our routines, pets and the man.

As long as she was hooked to bully sister Jane she had the strangest symptoms that remained unexplained.

The ultra-polite aren't nice. They lie to be courteous and that never works, it's the basis of hidden spite.

Being polite is basically lying. The fear of stepping on toes or being yelled at takes precedence: complying.

EVERY animal has boundaries, self-defense and emits feces. Bust my boundaries and I react quickly.

God help us I knew you'd start this but I'm way ahead now, a starlet and I'm not gonna take it so beat it.

Every time weakness/low self-confidence made me group up I was soon ruined by an unequal setup.

I was always excited about my "team" but soon found out I was the only one working and they were lazy.

They would allow in inferior ideas/compromising principals showing no constraint or "tolerance".

PEOPLE ARE CRUEL

I would spend most of my time arguing with them over theoretical laziness/not by the book enough.

Just be the best YOU can be and have a satellite around you of loyalists and keep it supple/recycled.

NO EVIL CONTRACTS

Never, EVER group with anyone. No evil contracts! The only one is marriage and that should work out.

A discovery is a part of nature and comes through a PERSON. You don't share it, you pay em.

I have a team and I pay em well. Just do your great genius work and wait to be discovered [God's will].

In the human world, a DISCOVERY is an actual structure in nature like a flower with beginning and END.

The discoverer may begin very primitive--an "ASS"--but becomes the BEST. It's an ARCHETYPE.

Archetypes are two-sided, always. You have the primitive and evolved. Switching to higher is the hero's task.

DIVIDE FROM THE CRASS/GROSS HERD

Divide from the crass and gross herd. They love their own, the others they despise (you're not preferred).

History shows: When a people get this immoral, total anarchy then tyranny follows. Repent, then flow.

If policies of selfishness, irresponsibility and immediate gratification rule a nation, all will be rationed.

People fail if susceptible to what's going on around them. Wear a hardhat: let nothing in, amen.

PEOPLE ARE CRUEL

Stop being a sponge to cultural crap. If moral you must stand separate and go by your own map.

With disrespect, negligence follows. Once trust is lost the whole thing rots and life's filled with sorrows.

We timidly conform to norms then are stung by evil bees, a swarm. Solution: privacy on a farm.

The left thinks if you don't smile like the other fakes, you're mean--cuz smileys cover all bad things.

It's good to be nice, but not if it means accepting every dirty habit, tendency, choice or vice.

The feminists would have done well in Nazi Germany: it was eugenics-based with abortions--many.

Say goodbye to those who won't see. Give up—you must--just to conserve your vital creative energy.

You can't herd cats nor coordinate individualists. They're the True Self, not mental midgets.

You can't trust someone if they're into the same evil TV and the weird things they hear and see.

NOT JUST DOING BUT CONDONING

It's not just doing but also condoning. Stand up against the terrible whether it be stoning or droning.

A vote for Trump was a vote for decency for look at the views of the enemy!

Progressive spirituality is defined as "non-dual consciousness"--but what a mess when evil isn't less.

The government's been in charge of "gender relations" for decades as our civilization fades.

PEOPLE ARE CRUEL

We're in a war and it's not ending soon--it's three generations of being rude/acting like buffoons.

Someone writes a book, they all use the same jargon and I'm supposed to take it as reality? None.

Realize there is a God. Realize Jesus is His Son, a doorway to save us from the horrible mess to come.

Big pharma drug reps are gorgeous supermodel prostitutes so compliant doctors get sugar to boot.

Coloring books by Big Pharma to induce kids to be sad to take pills to receive love from Dr. Bad.

Salon says pedophilia is good and the deputy Pope traffics children, take your pills and hail Satan.

I wanna know what's going on in the world, not just tell myself stories--how else achieve victory?

The insecure reflect groups and later are astounded--don't block these realizations (stay grounded).

People are either hot or cold--they either know or they don't. Regarding the latter, drop them and be bold.

FACE CRUELTY OR PAINT A FALSE REALITY

We live in times of great cruelty. We must prepare for this, not hide in projects painting a false reality.

Even though they're rich they're still sick and many evil people are still good-looking--think!

The women go along with gangsters and even enjoy danger but later realize it was better before.

Now here's a woman you should emulate. Not crazy liberal feminists who can't love/preach hate.

PEOPLE ARE CRUEL

No matter how bad it gets, God is above it so we should focus on Him whether in peace or the blitz.

Learn what's happening then trust God: Ignore what's all around: just wear the winner's gown.

You've overcome: Whether rum or slum you've come far above the dumb. Caution: it's everyone in sum.

It hurt when no one would listen. They felt pride as part of the system but now God'll get em.

The people have all gone crazy, there is no doubt. They allow this domino effect taking us out?

I have to blame someone and you were supposed to be watchmen but you allowed this evil end.

Liberals think if they don't like something it shouldn't exist, but you can't change reality—it's just a fix.

In the feminist matrix, "sexualized" means they're "superior". Not true—It just makes them weird.

FEMINISTS THINK IT'S COOL TO DOMINATE

Feminists think it's cool to be dominant. The weak always compensate for "feeling like a doormat."

Why try to copy men when we're already superior the way we are? Expand your femininity—be a star.

Women have never been so poor or abused. Feminism just sexualized females: used, and confused.

Liberalism is made of slogans, not substance. They can't know what I mean since there is no justice.

We could probably survive Obama, but not the foolish electorate that voted for the likes of him, to our end.

PEOPLE ARE CRUEL

There comes a time when you gotta give up on fools. Stop trying to convince those who just wanna be cool.

9/10 of people have no idea what's going on, and ten percent may know but still go along with the throng.

The contradiction: the feminists aren't against Islam as the abuser of women yet hate Christians.

So now we're going under judgment. Thanks to you trendies all morality is lost as we face ISIS armies.

Hippy attitudes of anti-Americanism, socialism and communism: stuck in the muck, bad luck.

Does this mean I'm a saint? Of course not--but we should all draw lines of acceptance vs. complaint.

They can't see. Their acceptance of the unacceptable is drilled in daily so now it's as deep as the sea.

Though you don't commit a sin, if you condone that same thing you're as guilty as sin, my friend.

THE NEW TOLERANCE MAKES US POWERLESS

The New Tolerance gives no allowance for moral prejudice and that's why they do it--to make us powerless.

You don't get to heaven by being nice. That's often just a smiley veiling emptiness--or perhaps a vice.

Tyranny is: Gangs and thugs roaming around reigning mayhem and terror on those innocent of error.

They run around imposing power to keep up the gravy train, not to catch criminals--that's what I disdain.

You sense their inferiority but they're the majority. Yet all people mourn when barbarity's in authority.

PEOPLE ARE CRUEL

We can get our country back—we can. "Secession fever" is taking over--it's the worse since it began.

"Love" is unconditional tolerance of what they want. They do selfish things while appearing nonchalant.

I know how they think, I was taught the same way. I bought the same trip but then saw the moral decay.

They disagree with you--and they're mean about it. Can't just discuss it logically, they scoff at it.

Many are immoral cuz they soak it up like a sponge. It is mindless and callous and makes me cringe.

Strange how the "loving" are tyrannical. This warped revolution to destroy truth is planned and methodical.

Never fear strength in numbers for God's man is a majority and through Him you have seniority.

NEW AGERS ARE INTELLECTUAL RUNTS

The new agers are intellectual runts. They've been given everything as gophers and false fronts.

A free spirit (hippy) is more easily infected and invaded than a rigid spirit so it's best to fear it.

Liberals are socialist, eugenicist control freaks--military camouflage in a bunch of creeps.

A thinker can't be controlled or he loses it. But that's what they want--don't take the bait, refuse it.

Lemmings don't produce--they're a joke--but the thinkers and fighters can't be unequally yoked.

Can tyranny be rolled back? If it can it all starts here since from 1776 we've had that knack.

PEOPLE ARE CRUEL

Realize that through self-development--the animating contest for liberty--we naturally overcome the enemy.

The prayers of one righteous man availeth much--so please keep praying God'll turn cold hearts.

Like all Hitlerians he takes a bit of truth and weaves in lies. He flatters, he smiles--while all liberty dies.

The lines are drawn, you're done. No more debating these dense fools, God has already won.

They ruin the whole country just for an experiment. It's all ideology so they won't debate, arrogant.

Cultural relativism says "it's all the same"--baloney. There's a hierarchy of humanity and the top is liberty.

Evil deals in secret meetings--nothing's above board. They lock you in but rescue's from the Lord.

NEW AGE UTOPIA IS REALLY HELL

The left's utopia is really hell. They paint themselves with loving colors but behind it's a bad smell.

The law isn't something to beat ourselves up over but rather gives discernment of others.

Why are women ruthless--cuz they've been held down for centuries? No it's because gone is all chivalry.

They'll stop at nothing to legitimize their ways. Make us all agree or even try it ourselves to be gay.

Founders said if we let morality go we may never get it back again. That's the way it works with sin.

Why must he/she see us pee? Why are they doing this--destroying all of our precious privacy?

PEOPLE ARE CRUEL

Take guns, target patriots. That's Obama, democrats and Hillary if she'd got in--lawless and treasonous.

Bring back what made America great: families, God, strength and Trump changing our fate.

Their goal is to destroy marriage, uphold deviancy by penalty of law and outlaw Christianity.

The fact he wouldn't help Christians while always helping Muslims makes us think he is one.

Political correctness shuts down debate and is marked by progressive wishful thinking/being irate.

Political correctness is a barrier to truth and a doorway to tyranny by silencing dissent by leftist orthodoxy.

Political Correctness dictates that language and practices that offend liberals must be eliminated.

I'm writing to friends as soon life ends: each minute we must study dangerous herd trends!

Between you and them there's no comparison. You can just float when fighting treason/lack of reason.

Think back to sixties minus hippies. People knew how to think and were thin and elegant, not so creepy.

GO WITH TRENDIES OR REALITY OF CENTURIES?

Think according to God's documents not to what's trendy. This gives direction and great prosperity (plenty).

In the sixties they drank like the Rat Pack on TV. Things catch on so from social hypnotism, flee!

To be trendy people make asses of themselves. Keep your eyes on standards not evil elves.

PEOPLE ARE CRUEL

One sin is condoning evil. You must repent for that too to become an eagle after being a weasel.

Ego marks societies going down: selfishness, sin, lust--addictions of all kinds as men are decrowned.

Liberals leave please. Make room for others willing and able to learn the un-sleaze with God to appease.

MORAL VIEWPOINT IS DIVISIVE: THIS IS GOOD

It's all about moral viewpoint: Do you see evil vs. good or is it ALL the same even with the hoods?

Leave behind bad ties--those your values despise. Then a grand vista happily opens after all those lies!

They'll block all views that challenge their own! Remember that to stay on top (on your throne).

The fact they're so angry shows how little they know. See it as a revolution as truth shows!

You'll find such peace if you just know you're right and stop quibbling with those quislings.

If you fail to draw lines you're no friend of mine. It's ALL about restraint and that makes us "fine".

A life on high with God shows continuous miracles and revelations. It's what we need as a nation.

In the midst of this terrible war He'll put you on the red carpet. Bank on this to just enjoy the moment.

Don't accept what you hear on TV, it makes you a dummy. You gotta study to know and it's not funny.

RESISTANCE TO GENIUS IS ENORMOUS

PEOPLE ARE CRUEL

Resistance to genius is enormous and deadening so your greatest potential comes from overcoming.

Born free, we had no idea what tyranny looked like and were unprepared when freedom took a hike.

Never support evil. They're on the other side--not equal. Be civil but this connection is lethal.

If they hate you is it cuz you told the truth? All they want is to be lulled into complacency, to be soothed.

It's just a herd. Conformists are not the True Self, it's all words. Superficial and silly is preferred.

Done to us: we're dumb and fat, too zombied to put up a fuss. But old vets will, feeling they must.

I thought it was the end. Evil triumphed over good, they have hearts of wood and no one understood.

Warning people is not hateful fear-mongering but me being friendly as a helpful watchman: amen.

LIBERALISM IS NOT FREEDOM

We're no longer free: We've lost our liberty as we go under tyranny--pure treachery and acerbity.

The clouds poured water, there was rumbling and roaring thunder and Your arrows went forward.

I know He's using me--God, that is. To get here I couldn't be so fattish and refused to be trendy or faddish.

Bible psychology overcomes all through repentance: History's cycles all show a good or bad sentence.

The haters don't care: they don't wanna hear it, they don't wanna know. It's all a trendy show with that foe.

PEOPLE ARE CRUEL

Distract, delay, deny: then later they say what's happening--a repeated tactic that's shocking.

On the razor's edge: it can go either way: We go into bondage or fight back as freedom saves the day.

We're right and they don't wanna see it. They shut you down, censure every sound: make money and they bleed it.

Though they died long ago they're still my family of Christian patriots and that's all I know--a family aglow.

To benefit them you must know you're right and they're wrong--must reject the liberal throng.

"EVIL DOESN'T EVEN EXIST"

The devil can be defeated by God but not if you won't even admit that evil exists--isn't that odd.

All it takes is knowing they're wrong and you're right--no need to get down in a mud fight.

Christian Restraint. We don't do things if God hates them--what sinners refuse to condemn .

Weak, spineless, stupid boring losers--that's our reps in DC. It's all special interests you see.

It's easy to discern: Whenever they call you "racist" you know who they are-- just say no, and turn.

San Francisco is filled with piles of defecation from liberal policies which are destroying a nation.

Take the day off and listen to Trump. First he'll deport the gangs and get us outa this slump.

The TV killer claimed racism made him pull the trigger. Divisive policies are the stinker.

PEOPLE ARE CRUEL

LIBERALS AND FALSE COMPASSION

Liberals and false compassion: tolerant of ISIS not Republicans, of deviancy not Christianity.

Liberalism is uber-tolerance, false compassion: feeling superior cuz they're "good" though fallen.

An epidemic of mental illness and being clueless.

Once you don't care anymore and believe any lie you become a delusional slob wanting it all to die.

Taught: "White males ruined minorities and America, parents and church are evil, " Not true, people.

"The flag is an evil sign of oppression" said the psychotic vermin who took over the schools since then.

It all started when you put a left-wing fanatic in the white house. Thanks a lot zombies, lush and louse.

Look at what liberalism has brought to this country. The ugliest, most unsavory debauchery.

Hollywood: Record low ratings, they're imploding.

We aren't doing/saying/thinking those things we're just living our own lives, scapegoats for your lies.

The entitlement generation: deserving of fame and riches just for being born, and very borin'.

THE WINNING SMILE IN SUPERFICIAL GENERATIONS

It's a "winning smile" which works every time in this shallow and superficial generation of mine.

We must stand together because in the end freedom will triumph over tyranny.

PEOPLE ARE CRUEL

We can still come back. 18th Century England was just as bad, spawning the Puritans in fact.

Conservatives will escape the cities to form pockets of liberty resurfacing in America's small towns.

Are Trumpsters turning against him to be part of the crowd, the dense flood of conformists so loud? Not

Go ahead and continue violence cuz you will do yourselves in. We're sick of this and proud Americans.

I'm not wasting one brain cell on em again. The liberals all around tho' it means solitude I guess.

Trump responded in one minute whereas Obama never responded darnit.

Nothing proves Trump's greatness more than his reaction to Houston which was in one moment.

Trump: best response in history across the board.

When they call you a racist never talk to the fascist.

GENDER AND MARRIAGE

Biology lesson: It's all about male and female, duh. Stay whole, they're just trying to mix us up.

They minimize their feminine side, to their detriment. For some reason "feminists" wanna be like men.

Females are victimized and vulnerable. That's why they need marriage: protection from the rabble.

The feminists are wrong. Women need protection, not social mingling or blending in with the throng.

Feminists advising divorce are just mad they're lonely and alone—they don't want you on the throne.

PEOPLE ARE CRUEL

Guard your marriage because being single sux. A happy home is protection from robbers and nuts.

Before marriage I was a target of nuts and neighbors but after, all problems dissolved like vapors.

You need someone in your corner. Marriage is the way for the supreme flowering of the female (armor).

The temptress is as bad as the whore. Modern women should be told: Don't tempt men, close that door.

Much neurosis is just copying someone you knew--one who followed the party line then left you blue.

UNDER STRESS THEY REGRESS

Under stress they regress by mimicking a relative and it's a mess since it's the sickest or one depressed.

Never consider suicide. I get down too but things always turn around soon after in God I confide.

You angry women are begging for pets to be slaughtered. You don't like thinking so but ya oughta.

You want my picture so you can pick me apart. Be above narcissistic culture or it's like the black arts.

They decide to target a group then local thugs go out and get em--that's how big gov is treason.

Women can be dirty to each other. This competition between females is getting worse not better.

Men tend to bond and help each other. Not females--no birds of a feather, just taking jabs: sever.

QUEEN BEES AND DOMINATRICES

The Queen Bee cuts everyone down to size. Especially the other females she

PEOPLE ARE CRUEL

seems to despise.

The angry wife makes everyone despise him. Men are hurt by broken families yet we aren't told of them.

Way back then when men were men they respected women--unlike today with forced "equality", amen.

We get dignity and power through chastity no matter what era we live in. Like fasting it creates wisdom.

They think it's cute to sin. They got it from blanch in the Golden Girls pushing debauchery, amen.

It's a shame I have to delete people due to rainbow pic. God made rainbows but this is sick.

Feminism stinks--it's all about killing your own babies and sleeping with the neighbor ladies.

Liberalism means "anything goes". No morals, lines or restraint--any barbarity's okay, you know.

Lascivious wicked witches are in control. It's all from political correctness and their loss of soul.

What America needs is a moral revolution and that brings prosperity for In sin we lose to enemies.

All they talk about is the joys and benefits of yoga. Why not just do it in silence if it's so good for ya?

WITH CRISES GO TO GOD NOT THE MOB

In disaster the small town happily comes together while before they never thought about the weather.

When faced with the strange clod I get into God and that's how I deal with the mob called "mod".

PEOPLE ARE CRUEL

Their time has expired, you're not looking to hire--for they're liars stuck in the mire and could start a fire.

Say it simply so there's no doubt what you mean. They've got A.D.D. and are hypnotized by fiends.

They're angry, just finding out what we always knew! That means we'll have protection for our novel views.

What else can we do but store food, relocate and then chill? We must stay calm until...

This event's a stroke of luck that makes you forget them: those who've minimized or ignored you, though kin.

Love it when he gets mad cuz he puts into words what I've felt for years about these liberal cads.

I can't say any more, Facebook will shut me down. All you need is below and other pages all around.

He's still a mindless pig: thief, scoundrel, scallywag and lowlife unconcerned about our hellish strife.

If those guys on stage don't talk about the police state--kills us, takes our stuff--what good are they?

Refuse to belabor the mud fights with candidates. Just know you're right about the alternatives.

The best plans of mice and men often go awry. When hope springs eternal, to tyranny bye bye.

GOD AND GUNS GO TOGETHER

New Agers don't see how God's word and guns go together: Restraint makes birds of a feather.

Most TV news is regurgitation from one news feed. It gets so boring and you don't need it.

PEOPLE ARE CRUEL

All through history Christians were called "haters" and that justified persecution by traitors and dictators.

Stop apologizing to this cult. If you do they'll hate you but if you don't they'll fade as a result.

Once the people were free of regulation, whole cities boomed economically--that's not an anomaly.

Like the early church, the fire of persecution fuels sudden growth of the kingdom of God.

Save yourself a lot of time--get "found time" by giving up lamestream news. They edit and omit--I refuse.

Cowardly Quislings: Traitors who hate America! We all have these in our family, for sure.

Friends and freedom fighters, ambassadors of Christ: if these people kill us I'll see you in heaven, Karen.

How is the war on Christians being waged? By calling them "haters of mankind" said the sage.

Save yourself a lot of time--forget FOX News. I suddenly added ten hours to my day, no blues.

They're taking us over and it's an evil script to get us in a grid and it's the end of liberty, no fib.

Pope is against executing murderers but not a word on killing babies. That should come first, crazy.

The pope is leading us to more central planning and less personal liberty for a start--and it's without heart.

ENVIRONMENTALISM SEEKS POWER

What of the pope's fake environmentalism? It's another way to get power through a tyranny take over.

PEOPLE ARE CRUEL

Government has the capacity to create, steer and stop storms and they'll take your guns.

So desperate for rescue we loved Trump (though he misspoke) with no thoughts we're unequally yoked.

Most murders are from knives--will they ban those too? It's totally stupid these points of view.

The entire nation is in "mass" hysteria--crazy over the pope-bouncer and his cronies who are phonies.

You won't like war. Gone are conveniences, nothing works, enemies get perks and you're never a star.

Using tragedy to push his gun agenda again, despite it being a gun-free zone that attracts em.

We're given a bunch of faux rights as our basic rights are taken away. This is tyranny, okay?

Liberalism hates conservative Christian views. All through history we're "haters" for our restraint and the loved are few.

An Authoritarian Kleptocracy: They're crooks and no one cares. Proof it's true: the Clinton affairs.

"We have no government armed with power capable of contending with human passions unbridled by morality and religion". John Adams

"Our constitution was made only for a moral and religious people. It is wholly inadequate to the government of any other." John Adams

IF CONTROLLED BY GROUPTHINK YOU'RE A WIMP

If controlled by groupthink, you're a wimp. This adaptation makes men cower and dumb women primp.

Doublethink says all things are true and simultaneously banishes anyone disagreeing with that view.

PEOPLE ARE CRUEL

Newspeak says my actions define who I am and if you object you're a hater and that's the whole story, amen.

"Offensive speech" on campus (says the crazy liberal view) are called haters, racists and bigots too.

Liberals are fakers: No original thought whatsoever and very disrespectful of thinkers.

They think they're smart due to "elite" schools but due to liberalism they're dumb/not truly cool.

So-called "altruism" is actually collectivism which is the worst kind of tyranny preventing optimism.

They know they're wrong: To cover that up they act more that way, confirmed by the throng.

The sin of the century is the loss of the sense of sin. Increasingly each day we are a trash bin.

"Don't tell me you're good, only God is good". That's what Jesus said to those with hearts of wood.

They preach "tolerance" but are only tolerant of those who agree with them. Liberal thinking: condemn.

DUMB OR BRAINWASHED TO HATE FREEDOM?

They're not truly dumb just brainwashed not to want freedom--they label that as slavery, in sum.

You need to know when to stop and when to go. Get outa there, man--what do these people know?

Trendies: power trips of arrogance and narcissism, If you disagree they accuse you of racism.

When a leader is surrounded by a spirit of familiarity, it's easy to lose clarity from this hostile polarity.

PEOPLE ARE CRUEL

It's just a herd. Conformists are not the True Self, it's all words and superficial and silly is preferred.

They're very clever: they wanna control it all with robotic levers so all loving ties are severed.

They say they're bringing lightness but really it's dark. The new illuminati: the trendies are sharks.

These people are sick. And they can be violent when just a little offended--yet thick as bricks, hicks.

People are socially needy cuz they've been told by the social culture that being alone is creepy.

They care more about that he offends than that he tells the truth--a social generation, the uncouth.

I don't care what they say about Trump, he rings our bell--others too if they're intellectual.

A dumbed down public is allowing this to happen. This was a longterm plan instilled like fashion.

Liberals can't face facts--it's all politically correct reality (women, blacks) giving us the axe.

We've so taken freedom for granted. When liberty is lost all goes to hell unless God has repented.

You're thinking these notions are yours? No, you've been programmed by the mind control corps.

POPULARITY: NO RELATION TO TRUTH

When a beautiful woman yells a gross shout she's like a flashing jewel in a pig's snout: no clout.

Without safeguards, government naturally becomes corrupt. It's just it's nature to obstruct.

PEOPLE ARE CRUEL

Popularity has nothing to do with truth. Wanting attention and many friends is all about the youth.

As bad as things get, always remember good overcomes evil--relieving stress over all those people.

I can't take it anymore! Constant bad news when life's so amazing: what a bore--close that old door.

When friends or family turn against you it hurts the most--all political, occurring from coast to coast.

When weak we act out other people's thoughts and habits. To avoid this regression, get strong.

When things don't work do not relapse into cultural images for approval-- these need removal.

They're so sophisticated you don't know you're being programmed and it's all entirely planned.

I'm no more for Carly--she supported turncoat Megyn Kelly and went against Trump our only ally.

They misunderstand cuz it's all lost in the superfluity of words. Terse verse is all that works.

UPPITY STARDOM SEEKERS

By seeking stardom they became uppity. Whereas they used to be bubbly now they just act snooty.

Vanity, futility, lies: it's all about the ME generation and we see the bad results in the family as it dies.

They're so full of themselves it makes me sick. In these tragic days they're hip but thick as a brick.

Wimps say "there is nothing that can be done, see?" Meanwhile they want some more for free.

PEOPLE ARE CRUEL

Can they get any more vain and self-involved? It's embarrassing--have we really evolved?

If you're always defending yourself in that particular group you must either repent, exit or have a coup.

PROMISCUOUS, FRIVOLOUS, DESTRUCTIVE AND INANE

Promiscuous, frivolous, destructive and inane: In these things there is no gain, they only drain (a bane).

It wasn't until after he got in that we realized all these things, so now the ol' liberty bell loudly rings.

When I was a feminist I was sickening. They all are when they take that narrative, a deadening.

As a conservative you'll see through everyone you ever knew. They were all taken in but not you.

Allowing them to define you, you don't know who you are. Now go within, repent of sin and be a star.

The best are trivialized in family and herd. They are scoffed at, walked on, dismissed or slurred.

Pictures, pictures and more pictures of themselves smiling. Sickening, it's all about social climbing.

Since "how not to be rejected or criticized" is their whole thing, of course they end alone or in a fling.

Don't make people bigger than they are, for people-obsessions get bizarre (sending many to the bar).

Free market with constitutional rights: that made us most prosperous but not now, gone is that light.

My favs are Bonanza and Big Valley. It's true Americana: strength, honor, liberty, individuality.

PEOPLE ARE CRUEL

Many are cold-blooded, others are hot. Being dense some can practice their trade but most cannot.

They're bigger than we are: With the power and means their "pain compliance" is even used on teens.

SOCIAL HARLOTS AND THE RED CARPET

Everyone thinks they're on the red carpet. FB gives that illusion as they seek fame: social harlots.

The "star": no different from any addict going down to turn around to become renowned.

If they're not against it they're for it--no lukewarm. It's a dividing line--separation works like a charm.

They act "tough" and "chic" but without worthy study they'll be up a creek cuz it's sick what they seek.

Give me a break! When those people become full of themselves it's all I can take: yikes—snakes.

They flit around to no good: the trendies: They talk like gangstas and it's all a fake (not truly friendly).

Merriment and enjoyment: God grants us this. But when all around is perversion, to God and Self it's a dis!

Newspeak says my worst defects are who I am and so if you criticize them you're no friend.

They've stopped judging anything at all. That's made them psychotic zombies and soon they will fall.

If you're not syrupy sweet, if you don't smile, if you just live your life they'll say "she's filled with guile".

NON-GENIUSES SEEK APPROVAL

PEOPLE ARE CRUEL

Un-geniuses follow the plan. They can't break out, they've sought approval since time began.

Avoid worthless and futile debate. You know you're right, you don't have to pick a bone with fate.

The ungodly are like flowers in a field, disappearing as smoke: Though they flourish, soon they're broke.

Only God gives self-esteem, not pumping ourselves up--for whatever you try you're still just a grub.

Since the female psyche screens out info from what they want to believe, they're easily deceived.

DUMB PUT SMART DOWN

The dumb put the smart down: they heckle, mimic and frown. Don't get rundown, you'll be renowned.

Stop arguing with idiots. It'd be better to stay silent for it's too tedious (since they are oblivious).

You'd get more from Bonanza then enduring the news. Just know it gets worse then avoid the blues.

We're social animals but to the extent one is not, he's on a different walk: it's deep thought not empty talk.

When it comes to guns, women need em more. That's why I can't understand the fem-trendies I abhor.

Don't fret when the evil flourish for soon they'll be gone. Though a swan, soon they'll be a bug you step on.

The wicked are like the beauty of fields: soon they vanish. Though evil is clannish it's still demolished.

Though beautiful on the outside, on the inside they are (dead men's bones and evil) Jekyll and hyde.

PEOPLE ARE CRUEL

To stay away from bad people, be a sleuth. They're often seen as the nicest and purist—that's the truth.

LOVE THE HOOD BUT HATE THE GOOD

I can't believe what idiots they've become. They're goaded to love awful things but hate the good—how dumb.

By resisting evil our spirits become stronger. This "animating contest" of liberty makes you younger.

I know how much it hurts to see your country get worse (as they lose their shirts)—pray and evil will disperse.

I know how much it hurts as evil gets the upper hand but by taking a stand God will take strong command!

We are shocked, in turmoil, sickened—but what can we do but turn to He who has always been true?

Getting ready for church (mod): Put on your armor against all things standing against God.

Panacea for all your ills: delete your rainbow friends. These are the weak who go along with trends.

Is it any wonder men have gotten sick of you broads? Button up and get some class—you look so odd!

If you condone something it's just like you doing it. Get that through your head sinner, stop confirming it.

Everyone's gone mad. They act tough but it's just a fad—the opposite to the era of mom and dad.

Who wants to spend time with a bunch of untrained, lewd children? Few mature, that is my wisdom.

They want you to suddenly become a dummy and agree with everything they say, or they betray.

PEOPLE ARE CRUEL

There is beauty and wisdom in traditional marriage and parenting. The anti-family fems are unrelenting.

How dare you cross these lines, you communist leftist wicca feminists: Think of the kids, you amoralists.

HATRED OF TRADITION IS DARK LIKE SLUM

They think anything new is good and anything traditional is misunderstood (lifeless as wood).

Smart in the land of dumb: dark like a slum. Rule of thumb: hold your head up high and don't succumb.

The left won't face man's depravity, as if it's all good. So they take lethal chances, never understood.

Hanging with lowlife is like wading in quicksand. It's too heavy and you'll be slammed--understand?

When not permitted to see, feel or express our grievances: what a mess for the aces = emotional illness.

They pick the best pics but don't look that way usually. Humans self-glorify while stuck in stupidity.

A nation of sheep shall be ruled by wolves. The dumbed-down won't hate the oppressor he loves.

Promises of conquest and grandeur: They'll do anything to be in the glare for all those voyeurs.

In the world of universal deceit, telling the truth is a revolutionary act. It causes rejection, in fact.

Are you social or deep? For there's a difference, a heap: Society only sees the deep as creeps.

Don't throw pearls before swine. For you'll be trampled: they're not benign (very bad combine).

PEOPLE ARE CRUEL

Soon it will all look like Detroit. They "progress" through destruction (for this they are adroit).

BORING LOQUACITY NOT DEEP THOUGHT

Boring loquacity isn't the same as deep thought, but many words are okay if you're finally saying a lot.

What they call the heart may just be gooey feelings they're told are smart (becomes a dark art).

They talk like they're so advanced while everything before now is attacked and they're against.

Up to forty I couldn't think critically and that made life prickly as I couldn't see evil (the epitome).

What happens if you're smart and they're all dumb? They throw you crumbs yet won't be your chum.

The irony: them thinking "liberation" means freedom to SIN which always results in the tyranny of men.

I hate how this pope says to ignore/stop spending on our pets. This is as sick as a commie gets.

Rather than complaining about your guests, stop sending invitations out. Just you: new route, no pout.

Dis-attend from most of what you see, it's a ripoff. Meanwhile don't trust many friends, they give tip-offs.

In this generation good is called bad, and bad good. Sweet is really bitter, and bitter sweet--understood?

Just why do you put up with these people, I ask? The desire to be "seen as social" is such a painful task!

It's a bad thing to be taken through your needs for flattery. Learn to see all impostors as in a gallery.

PEOPLE ARE CRUEL

When all have lost their moral compass and acting like an ass, repent and rise up as the new brass.

Make good use of your time by improving your mind. That's NOT Fox News (becoming a grind).

MEDIUM CHILL: CORDIAL BUT STEEL

Medium Chill: Cordial without letting them abuse you. That's how you treat liberals in the family or pew.

The very people assigned to protect us have been wimped by their angry wives. A sad situation, no jive.

Just because they're zombies doesn't make em harmless. Get involved with any one = no more calmness.

Though a "master", does he have wide-angled vision? Does he see the whole, does he have a mission?

When faced with toxic fury then sheepish conciliatory apologies: let them go, that's all you need to know.

Over-concern for looks marked Rome before it's fall: vanity everywhere yet none walked tall.

When we transcend chaos it always feels the same: extreme exhilaration as eternity is reclaimed.

If women are good to men the results increase a hundredfold. To a good man, a sweet female is gold.

We're supposed to go along with anything trendy though it means getting smutty and putting down daddy.

There is not one but two separate realities: Male and female--when the latter dominates, big penalties.

MESSED UP B WEAK MEN/ANGRY WOMEN

PEOPLE ARE CRUEL

They want us messed up by weak men and angry women. That's been the plan all along by evil vermin.

The utter cruelty in society is being downplayed. Everyone senses it but no one says it: it's all O.K.'d.

Some women are mad because they think they're supposed to be. When free of fake roles, they're free.

What is the best teacher? Having your faced pushed in the mud--a Ph.D. in the streets by Elmer Fudd.

Men are always apologizing for supposed anti-female slights. This is so sad too--it's just not right.

Stop being victims of pop culture wanting you degraded so the richest nation is brought low, glory faded.

RAMPANT MALE SUICIDE

38,000 suicides a year and 30,000 of them are men. The female victims have become the abusers, amen.

They're trying to remove all boundaries, leaving us in a cesspit of collectivism and immorality.

The ultimate goal of the toxic abuser is making you question your sanity. They rule reality, though it's inanity.

Stupid women tear their house down. In angry tears they drown when they coulda worn a crown.

If a woman is cruel and a man so wimped he can't be trusted, what is the child but self-disgusted?

They call it "tough love" but it's just being mean. Even the strong are intimidated by trendies: society's fiends.

I thought it was just me invaded by insanity until I asked and found you all have tolerated profanity.

PEOPLE ARE CRUEL

Just because one's rich doesn't make em good, sane or humane. But these elites rule in the main.

They don't want equality but privileges with NO responsibility. You must see this with your best ability.

IMAGE-MAGICIANS

People are about image not reality: they are image-magicians. For these types, stop fishin'.

Turn it all off and avoid those who scoff nonstop as you review all you've learned and now, the payoff.

God made all this and if they can't see it they have a stony heart. God made us too--soon we'll do our part.

The ego-driven narcissist sees only his own world, not the true external. Dense until death, the eternal.

When sin hardens the heart they get snippy, weird, mean: They become insensitive, losing their sheen.

If you take back a cheater it'll be worse next time, for in this generation they failed to draw that line.

Judge Judy is obviously anti-male. Women are gaining control, setting up sadly used men to fail.

Instead of letting em in and saying you're gonna be big why not be big and never let em in (and don't renege).

When chaos reaches critical mass you sense it's all gas. This marks your time has come: the new brass.

Nowadays the girl's are audacious and the boys timid. These are the trends, increasingly wicked.

Stop needing messages from the outer world. Stop looking and lurking: only God should be preferred.

PEOPLE ARE CRUEL

The way they eat is pure lawlessness. The outcome in looks and health is disastrous, so be cautious.

LOVE YOUR SPOUSE: IT'S A CHOICE

Love your husband or wife no matter what you feel about them. It's a choice not a feeling, amen?

I'm ready to rule. I've been through graduate school: bullied like a fool I found the true by being un-cool.

The victim constructs high walls against the whole world, as a wretched personality disorder unfurls.

Soon the victim hates everyone good or bad. He lashes out indiscriminately, seen as a wicked cad.

TV: As brainwaves and IQ's lower we go into a highly suggestible trancelike state--too dumb to be irate.

The victim begins to lose all boundaries. Desperate for love, the bad streams in (more subtle bullies).

The movies are all about revenge. This scratches an itch for the fringe: women having an edge.

Eagle-eyed and poker-faced: That's the look of tyranny as freedoms are erased and life debased.

Even in a rotten climate we can still make it. Just look UP (not down) then repent so God can bring it.

It's all about defending their sins which they love. You don't? You're out. Forgive, then be a dove.

Never apologize for power. It was hard work and grit making us the man/woman/country of the hour.

Is your style gangsta or your unique identity? That's once in a time, never before seen through eternity.

PEOPLE ARE CRUEL

Once she turns kids against father now she turns them against sister, boyfriend, aunt--whatever.

TRANSCEND LEVITY

Transcend levity. That's meaningless jocularity, not being a rarity. Life is serious so don't be petty.

Women aren't supposed to act that way (inferior). They were right and perfect before (superior).

We all know a good female role model. Just emulate her not the modern day rabble (they are awful).

When the fake talk they use too many words. All the wrong angles, the irrelevant or mostly just slurs.

Men, stop apologizing. It's pathetic you've been pushed this far but just repent and be uncompromising.

Most evil is social hypnotism: tolerating increased levels of perverse badness--that's new wave feminism.

Two causes of bullies: a tortured soul just wanting love or revenge/rage they can't let go of.

As people side against the victim he becomes an untouchable. How sad--aren't humans despicable?

The bullied begins to feel there is no hope. He loses all boundaries so as the sharks move in he can't cope.

Sometimes we stay when we should leave and visa-versa. Being where you don't belong causes inertia.

You never know one till you see him in all situations. Then you can trust with out surprise/degradation.

They don't care about human rights they only care how they're dressed: heartless and superficial pests!

PEOPLE ARE CRUEL

See yourself as the King (no cuss). You **MUST** lest you rust in self-disgust, mal-adapting to the lush.

What you see on TV is awful. Debauchery, licentiousness, betrayal and anything else unlawful.

THE HERD IS CONSENSUAL BLINDNESS

Never think popularity shows truth or rightness. More often it's bunk--the herd is consensual blindness.

Never judge value by how popular it is. The best thing the herd can't see--that's how good it is.

They fake "loving" to serve their gushing identity. It's not who they are at all, there's no real serenity.

We'll never be equal and thus communism implies tyranny: You gotta lop off heads to equalize you and me.

Feminine or feminist influence? Two separate things: one sings, the other destroys the home/has flings.

If you're great, expect hate. Envy is the reason for bullying so harden up but be kind (not irate).

People befriend victim just to use him some more. They get what they want then push him out the door.

They'll stop at nothing to buttress their fake ideas. It's all a surface party line cruel as North Korea's.

Having an inferior over you arouses jealousy of his power. Don't refuse to obey, soon it's your hour.

They say men die early due to their jobs--not. It's due to feminist insults, flings and divorce--rot.

SLAVERY WAS EVERYWHERE

PEOPLE ARE CRUEL

Slavery was everywhere. The biggest slavers were black but the white man freed the slaves: **DECLARE IT.**

The most targeted group is the white man, bar none. As he's blamed for all of it he is the one ruined.

The idea we're the most racist country--when we're the most open country in the world--is absurd.

Nine times outa ten it's them shooting each other but we're blamed for it. Look at the **STATS**, it's opposite.

High tech feudalism at the bottom with all us peasants and an elite at the top who is insuperable and distant.

How they start race wars: media primes us, Antifa goes out and burns stuff, media calls em heroes.

The George Soros plan is totally racist: paying young black men to go break stuff and get others to do it.

FEMINISTS ARE THE CRUELEST

Even as far back as the seventies this shit was starting up in universities and the feminists hated me.

I couldn't handle the cruel, rude, hateful and animalistic audience so went into solitude for decades.

Dimwitted celebrities may love limelight but fear of mass spite is what happens to conservatives, alright?

They were cruel to us and liberals in our families were **CRUEL** to us and that's the plain truth sis.

Liberals/feminists in our families banished/discredited us so we had no influence on the rest and we lost.

You see how cruel they are, what lady in her right mind would face that? It's the copy/after her death.

PEOPLE ARE CRUEL

Why does Soros/China hate us? Cuz JEALOUSY is the biggest human emotion: they want us dead.

China, Soros: One hand washes another cuza their common enemy, the American experiment.

THEY WANT US TO HATE OUR HERITAGE

They want us to hate our heritage. Though it was England and America who ended slavery, we're the targets.

The fate of American history is decided by the dumbest and least accomplished people in the country?

The extraction of money/property from people who never owned slaves to those who never were slaves.

Laws are the restraints that make us free. Ari Fleischer

For every conservative professor there are 30 America-hating liberals. This explains all of this, period.

So white supremacists are shooting down blacks everywhere? NOT, it's the opposite, hear?

Under socialism, those who run the government decide who is to get something and who is to wait.

This communism will be under the banner of "socialism" in a revolution triggered by supposed "racism".

It's a PROCESS of moving us into communism without us even being aware of it. Drip, drip, we're gone.

At the top of Black Lives Matter are trained Marxists. That's their ideological stance with Antifa.

To be "educated" means you must publicly denounce western civilization as the worst possible thing.

PEOPLE ARE CRUEL

Cultural Marxism has always wanted to take down western civilization along with Christianity, mainly.

MY GHOST TOWN

My life living alone in ghost town in the desert wilderness surrounded by 1000 acres for 26 years.

You'd never understand the peculiar way I had to adapt being misunderstood by liberals in the desert.

As time went on I became more peculiar and out of the mainstream. This triggered their scapegoating.

The youth wouldn't leave me alone but the old women got really officious in their small town gossiping.

The only way I stood it was from the long periods of total solitude in between thorny people problems.

They made me completely miserable every time they came and when they left I was always so joyous again.

Then a jealous female triangulated with neighbors against me. TROUBLE, anxiety--even out there, unfree.

The youth wouldn't leave me alone but the old women got really officious gossiping like any small town.

Through 26 years of living as a total recluse or desert rat you might say I was shaped a peculiar way.

PEOPLE ARE CRUEL

That's how the Potter forms us: by our adaptation to a problem environment presented to us.

Living that way was not near enough protection so I'd never do it again, now I have a high fence.

DIDN'T WANNA LEAVE A SHACK

When the day came to move to my mansion I didn't want to leave my shack. I was really attached to that.

When that rusty door closed on my shack I closed the world out and I reveled in eternity as a fact.

That sense of vast space/ETERNITY was so strong I didn't care if I lived in a dusty shack. It opened me up!

To this day I miss that place. What I have now is the greatest but an entirely different consciousness.

I found my heart, destiny, viewpoint and God in a shack and then in a minute it was all over, I was out.

People were jealous of my privacy way out there and were compelled to bug me, and what a bother.

Had to beg rides/put up with people's personalities. That's losing independence/being at their mercy.

Townspeople cast me as crazy preferring to live in a ghost town, separate from the flock, way out.

I had to live with all those projections from dumb liberals who could never understand me, and I was alone.

I think a couple of em woulda had me killed, just for being so different. Way out there? It's prairie justice.

And the two cops were influenced by Liquor Store Linda and she didn't like me, it was a bad scene.

PEOPLE ARE CRUEL

A lot of things coulda happened but didn't, under God's hand I was hidden. The whole time, protected.

UNWELCOME INTRUDERS

When the creepy liberals from town came to see me it was hellish. I just wanted them to leave or perish!

Even the church ladies were liberals by default. They really didn't know what they were talking about.

I'm handling success like a crate of eggs. Not making any sudden moves, going easy, slow and steady.

I saw a ghost town as very historical and it did something to my consciousness. A dusty shack no less.

Living in a ghost town--emotionally too--shaped my personality in peculiar ways, I'll always be this way.

There was NOTHING on the outside so I had to expand on the inside. My own inner journey, in private.

Tho' I had fallen to that level it was also something I needed in that era. All of life is in phases.

IT MAKES NO SENSE our government is allowing these vandals to rampage thru our country!

Finally in solitude, eternity took over. It filled me to the brim with the elements like rain on tin roof in winter.

A gambler knows the secret to surviving is knowing what to throw away and what to keep. Kenny Rogers

WRITERS AND ISOLATION

I can hear people yelling at me. That's the human world and introjects from a past era of treachery.

PEOPLE ARE CRUEL

Of course I lack confidence the devil held me down for years. I'm just a writer/don't wanna go out there.

The last thing Aunt Grace said was "NEVER chase a man". That was the most important bit of information.

Fear of exposure, body dysmorphia, shyness, call it what you want--the very thought of it is just too much!

I'm a writer, I'm eternal--I don't have to be seen. I am known through my words as in past worlds.

I've been through ENOUGH having my face pushed in the mud by the rabble and the duds like in Chad.

I WANT CLASS AND VALUES

I want you--high class with values--and ONLY you and am willing to wait until destiny changes our fate.

You can see I'm stuck but conservatives aren't reckless, I'm confident you know this. Thanks for your patience.

It's something I have built up and accumulated in this life and I'm willing to share it with you as a wife.

It is said female genius comes to success through her home. I believe this to be true, it's the all.

There are fifty thousand of these quips [twoliners] and I don't question it, it's just what I do naturally.

Maybe someone will read em, maybe many will read em after my death, I don't care--it's just what I do.

It's as natural as a bird singing and comes after a lifetime of social overcoming plus also familial lunacies.

What am I? Well a big part is my daily routines from lessons built up. What I am is a composite.

PEOPLE ARE CRUEL

I've done my work now I'm gonna enjoy homelife to the max and wouldn't think of going out there/hexed.

You've helped so many people there is no reason you can't go to the top now.

A sea of words, I've been called to do it. But it doesn't overwhelm, daily I escape into views/music.

At times God leaves me to test my faith in the dark. Those are hard days but then He's back tomorrow.

ONE LITTLE [HUGE] LIFE CHANGE

Don't take their advice about diet. Just eat the way you think after learning all the rudimentaries.

So you're a rawfoodist, now no fried broccoli. A vegan, no more butter. A 811er, no avocado either.

Refuse the labels and eat by instinct. As natural as God made it/once in the day, now be creatively lit.

They'll tell you not to drink bottled fruit juices/not do this or that. Read some tips/learn about good fats.

Processed starches nearly killed me. Back to fruit and fat and all of that, no more biscuits feeling acidy.

I tried eating Americana--pancakes with butter/syrup--and just got sick cuz I'm one of the hypersensitives.

The last time I ate bread with butter and jam I never felt such pain. Hours later, here it comes again.

Fruits and veggies go alkaline and ALL ELSE GOES ACID and that explains your acid reflux, I'm sure of it.

Ehret said it last century: EVERYTHING but fruits and veggies causes acid, does this not explain it?

I grew so sick of the constant presence of esophageal acidity I was willing to choose foods differently.

Acid reflux, allergies may not inflame till ten hours later. It's too much of a gamble, be a fruit fat faster.

I'd go for a green smoothie for breakfast if it meant I'd never have acid reflux, a constant presence.

Acid reflux: an American malady and constant tragedy as we think "here it comes again" excruciatingly.

A bulimic can suddenly discover that fasting [austerity] has greater benefits without the terrible drawbacks.

He'd always been an indoor man since Viet Nam. I got him outdoors more and he's again a healthy man.

Music is the most evocative, opening up worlds inside. I must always remember this: wisdom applied.

BASIS OF AMERICANA: RIGHTS

What is the basis of rich Americana? To protect the rights that God gave us. Bill Lockwood

It is very clear now the GOP want's nothing to do with the neocons or RINOS = 97% are in the know.

America's greatness is BASED on individual choice and accountability not a giant collectivity.

Ignominious mediocrity and poverty of soul is the result of putting the collective over the individual.

Outlawing private facilities for women/girls so there is NO SAFETY or privacy in bathrooms/showers see.

Trampling on our rights under the false name of "equality" and they will take the kids if we object see.

PEOPLE ARE CRUEL

To quote Thomas Jefferson this is about Tyranny Over the Minds of Men, a black cloud controllin'.

Those who are trying to stop the whole country from breaking up are labeled domestic terrorists.

HYERSENSTIVITY UPDATES

Delete grains [grainsludge/anti-nutrients] or nightshades [tomatoes/spuds] for painful acid-reflux.

One gets so hyper-sensitive he ends only on fruit to prevent extreme pain from foods denser.

Grains produce grain-sludge in the intestines, grains have anti-nutrients--who needs this?

Grains poke holes in the gut producing fecal blood and stomach aches like you never thought.

No grains, no gut aches. What a relief! No spuds no gut-aches because they're nightshades see.

Bread you just eat, same with crackers. Who needs the rest, across the world it's bread, no matters.

After your starch-only breakfast just fruit for lunch in salads, juices and smoothies or such.

After your fruit lunch just skip dinner. It's ridiculous to eat at night then choke in your sleep, a goner.

HAPPY UPDATES

Soren Kierkegaard Tombstone: Now I sleep in valleys sweet, just with Jesus will I speak.

Once you bring it up, face it & self-forgive it's a mere drop in the collective subconscious of all time.

I don't wanna pump myself up with pics/profiles/lies but just to produce and let them decide.

One reason for retirement is to be protected from mean ageist comments from the rude/common.

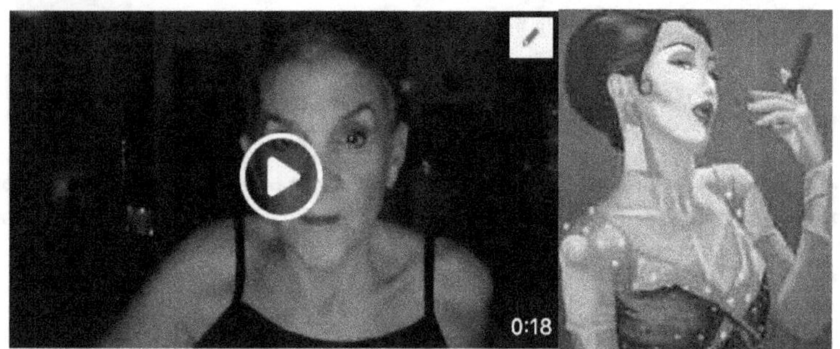

THE HERD IN WORDS
HIX POLITIX
HOW THEY RUINED US
JUST SKIP DINNER
LE FEMME AND THE COMMUNIST SPIRIT
LIBERAL CHAOS & ROT
LIBERAL DOUBLETHINK
LIBERAL GALL 1 & 2
LIBERAL SHOVE-DOWNS
LOCK YOUR GATE
LOSERS and Femme Fatales
MANUAL FOR SUPERIOR MEN
MODERN ART FROM HELL
MOSTLY FAKE
NOTES TO CHAMPS 1 & 2
OVERCOME FRENEMIES
PC MAKES US CRAZY
PEOPLE ARE CRUEL
PEOPLE PROBLEMS 1 & 2
PERSECUTED GENIUIS
POLI-PSYCH MYSTERIES
PRETENTIOUS SLOBS
QUEEN BEE
RED NEW DEAL
RETURNING TO FIRST NATURE
SEASON OF TREASON
SEPARATE MEANS HOLY
SOCIAL HYPNOTISM
SOLITUDE SOLUTION
SUPERCILIOUS
THE SCHOOLS SCREWED EM UP
TOAD TO PRINCE
TRIALS CYCLES
TRUMP VS. GROUP
TRUST IN TRASH
THE TRUTH ABOUT PEOPLE
UNDERHEANDEDLY CLEVER
WALK TALL WITHIN WALLS
WE'RE NOT ALL ONE
WINNERS SKIP DINNER
WORK OR SMERK

KAREN KELLOCK PH.D.

Karen Kellock received her Ph.D. from University of California, Irvine and was a postdoctoral fellow at the Medical School, Dept. of Psychiatry [NIAAA and NIMH grants] to develop a theory of System Pathology: the Debris Theory of Disease, presented in 120 books and 22 textbooks for the general public. The theory has a general formula: All disease is obstruction, all recovery is elimination, all success is attraction. The three obstructions are people, habit and food. Remove your obstruction and snap to your goals, waiting in the wings.

www.ingramcontent.com/pod-product-compliance
Lightning Source LLC
Chambersburg PA
CBHW061724250726

48657CB00002B/753